The Latest Winter

About the author

Maggie Nelson is a poet, critic, and award-winning author of *The Argonauts*, *Bluets*, *The Art of Cruelty*, *Jane: A Murder* and *The Red Parts*. She lives in Los Angeles, California.

The Latest Winter

MAGGIE NELSON

ZED

This edition of *The Latest Winter* is published by arrangement with Hanging Loose Press, 231 Wyckoff Street Brooklyn, New York 11217-2208, USA.

www.hangingloosepress.com

This edition published in 2018 by Zed Books Ltd, The Foundry, 17 Oval Way, London SE11 5RR, UK.

www.zedbooks.net

Typeset in Haarlemmer MT by seagulls.net
Cover design by Alice Marwick

A catalogue record for this book is available from the British Library

ISBN 978-1-78699-469-1 pb
ISBN 978-1-78699-470-7 pdf
ISBN 978-1-78699-471-4 epub
ISBN 978-1-78699-472-1 mobi

for Mark

Table of Contents

Acknowledgements

Some of the poems included here first appeared in *Delmar, Fell Swoop, Fort Necessity, Hanging Loose, Open City, Shiny,* and *Heights of the Marvelous: A New York Anthology* (St. Martin's Press, 2000).

Many thanks to the very necessary ladies of *Fort Necessity*; to Rebecca Reilly, for her unerring eye and ear; and to my friends at the Graduate Center at CUNY, Wesleyan University, and the Great Jones for their support throughout the writing of these poems.

I.

The Poem I Was Working On
Before September 11, 2001

after Louise Bourgeois

Say something awful, say
"She leaned on the fork"

Say something beautiful, say
"Eyes smudged with soft kohl"

Now lead the way under
the spiders, yes under the spiders

where a bad woman rules. Glassy
white eggs in a wrought-iron

grid—she almost goes through
with it. Engulfed in a perfect

day, the pressure lifts—
urban life is OK as long as

there is still wind, something new
to breathe, though do you want

to know what that strange smell is
Well I'll tell you it's the fumigation

of the lizards in the subway system,
KEEP CLEAR, DO NOT INHALE

O you're so gullible. But can I breathe here—where?—
in this tiny circle, where the homunculus

is hopping on the gamelan and playing
the song of joyful death—just think

3

about that. Say something nice, say
"Your sexiness is necessarily an aporia,

but that just means nothing can ever
demolish it." Now that we're grown up

and have no willpower (of all things!)
The absurdity is I hope this will never, ever end—

not the banging on the can, not the dark brown liquid
in the blue glass. I love it here, on earth—I don't care a fig

for what comes next, which is exactly what
the suicide bomber said of the Israelis he killed yesterday

at the discoteque. There is something bestial
in me, it wants to be drunk on saliva, and

there is something ugly about me, which has to do
with my fear of dying of hives. But above all

there is something very lovely about today,
the day I wandered beneath a great spider

and the city opened itself up as if to apologize
for its heat and changing ways.

Don't sit there slobbering all over
the thermometer! The least you could do

is try to capture an enigma with an image,
or don't sweat it—out West my mother

is fondling the stone bellies of the Three Graces.
She waters everything at night now, she is

4

the night-gardener, she goes out with a flashlight
and looks for insects doing their deeds. Looks

for all that oozes underneath. Yesterday I saw
a man burn a strip of skin off his arm—

he just threw the skin in the trash
and for a moment we all stood there, staring

at the bright white streak on his arm. It didn't look like
anything. Then the red blood started to perk up

around the edges, it was quite eerie and beautiful,
it was the skin under the skin, it was

the flesh. Our flesh is often so red
in the photos that get taken of us, and I admit

that something about life overheats me, but nothing like
the teenager who overdosed on Ecstasy and was found

on her kitchen floor with a body temperature of 104 degrees.
I saw it on the News, the News whose job it is to scare me.

It would seem by such a lead story that
these are decadent and peaceful times, but there is

much else. But the rest doesn't count. The bottom half
always drops out, as George W. dines along the Venice canal.

But today—just today—I felt new for the first time this century—
no one noticed me—I was unsexed!—I stood

in front of *Les Demoiselles d'Avignon;*
I could take it or leave it. I read Dr. Williams

in the park, he says the sun parts the clouds
like labia (I guess he would know). Looking up

from my book I became momentarily afraid
of the polar situations that may arise between us,

but then I let it all go. I'm tired of small dry things.
I want to nestle into the clammy crack

between conscience and id—speaking of which,
I'm so glad you turned me on to donut peaches—

they will taste like this summer until
they taste like next summer, but why

think about that yet? You never let me see you naked
but when you do it is like a rain of almonds, your soft spots

smell so tart and floral, and you don't pull me into you often
but when you do you pull me into you. All of this

is worth fighting for. We may be called upon
to do so, in which case there will be no more Ovaltine,

no therapy, no crackers. Praying is just thinking
about nothing, or trying not to think about

the lines of cows, their fat nipples squeezed
into the machines. (I'm surprised the milk

still comes out!) Through a hole in my head I imagine
my brain seeping out, in shell-pink ribbons

as the village moderates itself into night:
bottles are getting recycled, objects are left behind

in moving vehicles, people remove their earrings and war-paint
and get ready to sleep. Tomorrow is Saturday,

and the city will rise. There could be a planet out there
whose inhabitants are watching our demise, but enough

already about the living dead! There may be
neither space nor time in the space and time

in which I love you, and thus our love
will remain iridescent forever, and have only

as much sternness as the universe has to offer
(which may or may not be much). There *is* a world

that I think, but it is not different from this one.
The great spider and her shadow, the clouds

moving across the mirrored Cineplex—they're real, too.

Twin of sheen

Twin of sheen
Sit with me tonight
Tell me all you've seen
Your monsters bright
Your shapely disease
Stay until day
Promise to be
Thickest with me, bathe
Me in the sea-smell
Of your flood
Your little hell
Your little hood
Your sly walk
Your aching thought.

Brightness

I like a pinto bean now and then
words rattling in a cage
a light show in a jar

Back at the bakery they said
you were bright and so you were
a menu of striped sky-blue sky

Stranger in rage, shall I sweep up
after the bogus orality,
the spidery rasping on my walls

As for you, you must choose
the best jacket
for your new life on the street

As for me, I've got to get a sense of comedy
about the deep fruit in which we're living
raspberries dribbled on fresh slices of paper

You just came and took it,
took it out of me like a tonsil
Oh you, prodigy you, and all your sweet mashed potatoes

1999

In my dream last night
I had a boob job
and my nipples were
pointing off in two
different directions.
It was disorienting
and the photographer
was disappointed.
But later he turned into
the best lay of my life
He was so huge
to get inside me
he had to hoist himself
onto a sort of cross-country
skiing Nautilus machine,
at which point I was
part new boob girl,
part Christina Ricci.
Upon penetration
everything exploded—
he exploded, I exploded
the dream exploded
I didn't even remember it
until you grabbed my breasts
in the living room and said
What kind of bees
make milk? (Boo-bees.)
Why is that joke

always funny to me,
as is the one about cheese
that's not yours (it's
Na-cho cheese!) but that one
needs Pookie to say it
out loud. But back to
my main concern:
what are academic thoughts
and how do you know
if you have them?
Everyone at the lecture
was talking about
the Gerty chapter in *Ulysses*
while I was spacing out,
trying to remember
if I'd seen it illustrated
or just dreamt it—either way
I can still see the sketch
clearly, looking up her
blue dress, a red band
of elastic stretched taut
across her crotch. It would be
just like someone to illustrate
that scene. Thanksgiving
is almost here, what shall
we eat? My mother is
coming over for dinner
but sometimes we don't agree
on things, for example
she says when I was growing up

I wasn't pretty, I was distinctive.
But everybody knows
distinctive is code
for ugly. The thing is,
I wasn't ugly, though
an oral surgeon once
told me so, but now I know
he just wanted to
rearrange my mouth.

Train to Coney Island

This time I'm going all the way to the Mermaid Parade, I only wish
I were a photographer! It's late, I hope the floats won't be dismantled.
Last night I dreamt that L. and I got married but our audience
was not behaving—Jennifer Miller the bearded lady kept yapping. In real life
I splintered up and asked M. for a second chance: "I'll change," etc.
We are all equally deceived, perhaps, by ourselves. One thing I know for sure:
it's pointless to hope I have an encyclopedic mind. All it ever retains
is the bare-bones sentiment of the thing, the hiss of information
rushing off into the canyon. I don't really mind, words chip off the block
and float in summer air. They're nothing compared to the buttery rings
of Saturn! & I have always been a sucker for mystification. Here we are
at Neptune Avenue! It's funny and a little sad that I've written such a chatty,
prosy sonnet, as all I wanted was to take the train to its final destination
and write a teeny chiseled poem, some perfect illumination

Blockbusters

for L. Menand

Blockbusters are only
blockbusters if we
go see them, so let's
go, let's make them
what they are, let's
pay for them.

the future of poetry

the poetry of the future has got to have a lot of nerve. it's got to come from at least three brains: the brain in the head, the gut-brain, and the brain in the ovaries. it will wax red and rise bone-white. the poetry of the future will be nutritious and opulent. justifications for its existence will no longer be interesting: lenin loved beethoven. the poetry of the future will glitter like a scimitar. the poetry of the future will be unabashedly adolescent. it will get younger as it gets older. it will reflect the interests of both carnivores and herbivores. it will be as heterogeneous as it is misguided. the poetry of the future will watch blue branches shaking in winter and red canyons gaping with sun. it will send a space shuttle full of representative poems to a gaseous planet where upon exiting the shuttle the poems will turn into gorgeous multicolored rocks that can live without water. the poetry of the future will wear squeaky shoes in the vatican. it will say where we work and who we love and what we eat. sometimes it will be hungover and desperate. it might bite its nails. tired of being on the lam, it might have to choose between giving itself up to the authorities or going out in a blaze of glory. the poetry of the future will be so enormous that it will only be visible from an aerial perspective. many will believe it to be a message from aliens. the poetry of the future will be so expensive and in demand that it will disrupt the global economy as we know it. as no one will ever be fully awake to the miracle of our existence its work will never be done. sometimes the poetry of the future will have to put on a silk kimono and sigh.

sometimes it will need to fuck like a bunny. other times it will have to walk 29 miles to visit a grave. it will have bones to excavate and houses to rebuild. the poetry of the future might worry it will die from weeping. it might have to send a root down to come up. sometimes it will put on a head-lamp and go looking for urchins. at times the poetry of the future will be nothing more than red eyes caught in a flash photograph or the memory of percussion. the poetry of the future will compete with advertising and lose. it will then be run by a secret society of cave-fish that have never needed to develop eyes. it will retreat to a hearth made of mud and eat beans with its family in a comfortable silence. the poetry of the future will be the last sad sack to leave the party. the poetry of the future will be written by women. it will accept chance as its engine. it will have a front row seat at the cinema. it will be vigorously imperfect. the poetry of the future will live in a redwood tree for 2 years if it feels it has to make a point. it will understand that seeds must stay scattered. the poetry of the future will say, last stop, everybody off! once we get off the poetry of the future will set us on a scavenger hunt in which the first thing we have to find is our own idea of utopia. the poetry of the future will come home sopping wet after thinking things through and ask for a second chance. the poetry of the future might take a vow of silence. the poetry of the future will know everything there is to know as soon as it is born. above all, the poetry of the future will do whatever the hell it wants.

my life as an exchange student

for puri y las gemelas

teenage girls in the style of "heavy"
dance with their faces an inch from the wall

I am a virgin in the way
that hurts, and life feels consistently

intense: the tan face of danny
at la cuadra, he seems so worldly

the streaked hair of the town slut
who is on "la pastilla"

I am not on la pastilla but all the same
they will eventually call me una desgracia

(how would he know, my spanish father
who worked all day at renault)

those were the days of pepper trees, when
I was unsure if anyone would ever love me

and afraid I would die of acne
in a foreign country. each dusk I waded

in the ankle-high cotton that floated in
from portugal across the fetid river

where we weren't allowed to swim
(it had something to do with franco).

I didn't die there, though I could have
or later swirling underwater in the dirty

mediterranean, all fucked up on sherry
after giving first fellatio by a hotel pool

(not our hotel, we'd hopped the fence)
we woke up on lawn chairs in the mist

I don't really know if any of this actually happened
or who those guys with the self-inflicted tattoos were, anyway

ever since then I'm a little afraid of madrid
I was jealous of all the girls, their beauty

the brunette from L.A. and my botticelli angel, amy
I thought a lot about free will and siouxsie

who would have thought
my future friends would be

so percussive, that I would live so long
in one american city, or that I would learn to like

the dick stuffed in my face.

Holed Up

Holed up in my room with the Puritans
They woo me with their vigor and eye for detail

but still I schlep Roman for icons of cloud out
my window, ominous gray then shouting gold

then dispersed into an archipelago of dust
As night comes and closes the shops that sell

cashmere scarves outside my price range
strollers roll by stuffed with extra children

Everyone is stocking up at the deli, there's a certain piracy to it
I think it's the streets that first make the sound of rain

Unbridled honesty, is there any other kind? Oh yes
I used it yesterday, when I half-told you something small

Juliet

(after Eve, with a last line by Lee Ann)

I am lying on the bed which is really
just a mattress on the floor that smells
like incense and like Berkeley

Glass sliding doors lead out to a stone patio
and a kidney bean-shaped pool that glistens
in the early evening light, he is standing

to light a candle and find a condom, he is
short and white and Irish with freckled shoulders
and long hair down his back like red wheat

What he doesn't know is that I'm on a mission
and he's the one I've chosen, this time
I'm quite ready after spending the afternoon

lying around like cats in the sun
his breath hot behind me
Do you like it like this, I like it like this

You see he was teaching me, we had
the same size bodies but I was sharper
around the edges due to my critical eye

It was crucial that he had both
a verbal and visual imagination
His skin so blotchy red color rising

in his cheeks in patches, his eyes an astonishing blue
and always red-rimmed because he was such a stoner
I lay on my back amazed and perplexed

especially by his urging *You've got to find the rhythm*
I don't know if it felt good it felt like young animals
thick in red and gold and darkness

Afterwards we went swimming and then sat
in the hot tub where he said he was hard again
and I was sore and steaming and we did it again

and then again. Later I would let him
videotape me masturbating but
I would only do it under the covers

so all you could see on tape was a moving mass
of white comforter. In another part of the tape
I am sitting naked, looking shy and giggling uncomfortably

as he sprays water on me from a spray-bottle
probably just trying to get me to move around but
I couldn't move, I was too excited and too sad

and too anxious to see what would happen next
which was that his father drove me to the BART station
winking the whole time, saying *Now I know*

to leave my boy alone when I see your bug parked outside
A few days later I have to go visit my sister at a reform school in Idaho
and end up spending Christmas in a teeny rural hospital

with what I suspected was a punishment from God, so much red blood
in my urine and pain in my abdomen, but it turned out to be
what my mom later called "the honeymoon disease." And while I was gone

he fooled around with my best friend, and thus I was betrayed
by the boy who never loved me the way I wanted to be. Still
it was my mission, my wetness, and my sadness

My fifteenth year, drunk on the drug of love

Lucia

Her skull was
undead, put together
like the skin of

a grapefruit, mocking
the whole grapefruit.
I made the mistake

of touching it:
it came apart, like
a soft planet.

The ghouls of the dorm howled.
I've got to wrap it up
in two black garbage bags

then pretend I never
found it. Frantic:
the skin of the grapefruit

pocked now with a piercing
and a worm of blood glistening
against the velvety-white interior

Off-white, really, but no exactitude
of color will alter the collegiate
setting, nor the horror.

Poem Written in Someone Else's Office

Bare fingers,
trees. Four
blackbirds in
one, four

mistakes. The
mistakes my mind
makes, all
one hundred

and eleven miles
it takes to get
here. Now what's
that sound—a buzzing

and a whimper,
pipes waking
up from sleep—
so much like a

dying animal
I check it, thinking
Squirrel, don't die
on me. Not in here,

in this office
that's not my
office. This is
the office of

a woman who
picks up pencils
from time to time
and makes a

sketch, like
the abandoned
portrait in the
corner. If she

doubled as
a shrink that
would help explain
the tissues and

the couch. I lie
down. I could
live here forever,
why not. Four

mistakes: I drove
here. They gave me
a key. The office
is bigger than my

bedroom. Can I
sleep in it? I'm too
afraid to ask.
I'll just sneak

in my wine and
toothbrush, curl up
on the gypsy rug
and stare out at

the chimney-tops
of this mumbling
town. Right now
the ground is all

crusty from
yesterday's snow;
sun peeks out
onto brick. They

promised it would
be like this—each
day better than
the next. My sister

tells me she always
misses our father
today, on the 18th
anniversary of

his death. I want
to call her but
I don't know how
to dial out. Shall I

go out for Italian food
by myself, then
wander around
with crumbs hanging

from my lips?
This woman's got
files and files on
books—mostly on

Victorians, lots
on Virginia Woolf.
And her husband
is somehow related

to the creator of
that French elephant
Babar, or maybe
he is the creator

himself, I really
don't know or care,
but his picture
is everywhere—

balding in that
crescent shape,
kind eyes. Kind of
how you'd expect

someone's French
husband to look. If
it were my office
I'd hang a photo of

Patti Smith to make
me feel better about
pissing in that cup.
Darkening room. Blue

shadows, nothing
quite real—like
the fresh-faced girl
I had in here earlier—

"Have a seat," I said,
as if it were my
couch. But I am
the teacher now, though

I brought a yellow
thermos I call
"The Rabbit"
from Chinatown

and spilled green
tea all over the
rental car seats.
Last night I dreamt

the whole solar
system revealed
itself to me, first
the moon and its

soupy craters, then
Jupiter with its
red storm-spot,
then Saturn with

her gray eyes.
Somehow I knew
the planets were making
themselves visible

out of sheer
generosity, as if
they had decided
earthlings were just

too sad, wafting about
in space, feeling so
alone. So they made
a one-time show

of pity and luminosity
that I was lucky
enough to see. It's
true, I really am

too verbose for
you, and I have known
all along that
words will not do.

I am apart in a
made-up way.
Days like today,
all I want

is for someone
to come by with
a fat rubber ball.

Goodbye to All That

I went back to the source of it all
The dried leaves made noise
There were many houses for sale

and winter shadows of wind chimes
on porches. I was snooping around
pilfering frozen candles from the yard

when a guy came out holding a small baby
No you don't, no you don't
I used to live here, I lied, then fled

I don't know what I was looking for
so I don't know what I found
The steeple's still turning from black to gold

Groups of children in parkas still go
to the Fiesta Market, babies still sit
in strollers encased in plastic

It's just that I've missed the birds
so much, the seagulls flying inches
above the whitecaps, black

in silhouette against the western sky
There were tears, loose and streaming
from the cold and heart, then a very cold wind

gusted my scarf off my body, wrapped it
around a wire, then let it fall
to the ground, where from a distance

it looked like a small dog. Even if
I return, I know I won't be back
now that it's time to say goodbye to all that

II.

29

It's come to this, and I'm glad
a vanilla Toyota on the Sprain Parkway
then a bath in the inimitable silence
The tub is clean, cleaned surely
by industrial agents
I have new hipbones, new veins
new tiger scratches on my thigh
three jagged lines, iridescent
against the muted autumn bedspread
which is shiny and water-repellent and full of fruit
On TV Britney sings, "I'm not a girl,
not yet a woman," and I too feel very much
neither, and will probably feel thus forever
in a winter which is amazingly
mild, but still there are no leaves
only the evergreens and the pavement
that talks to me. Last night I had a dream
I was wearing a tank top
and a low-waisted "ethnic" skirt
You said, quite casually, your breasts look beautiful
in that thin white shirt. I felt very beautiful,
we were standing on a street corner
which was not New York, probably the Haight-Ashbury
of my birth. It was so sunny. Cars drove by,
fumeless. Now the overcast sky is vanishing
and a pale blue appearing

All this before ten a.m.! A cup
of bad Lipton tea finishes me
It is quiet, so quiet, and there are three
mirrors, all of which reflect my smudged
mascara, a hotel woman on the verge
Except that I'm on the wagon now,
haven't you heard? That particular darkness is
spent. All because of a low, bright humming
in the root of me. 29 years
of a small life. Still I haven't learned
how to die, but there's time. I wake up
with my mind a naked magnet
about to be bearded with the shaggy lead
of my thoughts, I find it funny
that they come back to me as if
they're mine, that sleep hasn't washed
them away, blue-rinsed this litany
of detritus. I hear it as if I'm standing
behind a Japanese screen, chuckling
at what pretends to be me
Little spiny trees, gray needles
pointing toward the nothing-
ness of the sky. A row of cars
parked outside, none of them
mine. Seven minutes now
past checkout time.

Imagine

The world is so full of things
you could never imagine

An old man brushing
what's left of his hair

with a plastic fork;
a Hasidic guy pushing a stroller

full of frozen poultry. Then
a postcard bearing cherry blossoms

arrives in the mail
It says that you love me

Birthday Poem

It's been so long
since I've written
you. Today
October came
and frosted up
my windows
prematurely, I
sat inside
wearing two
sweaters
watching big
blue clouds
dominate the
sky as the sly
orange sun
sopped the
tops of the
stubby cornices
on my block. I
thought about
writing you
then, but
instead I
went out
and mailed
a letter and
bought two
rolls of toilet

paper. I saw
the moon just
starting to
rise, about
¾ of it, so vast
and know-
ledgeable, swept
clean by the
cold. I thought
of the space
show I just
saw, where
they flew us
past Io, one
of Jupiter's
moons, whose
surface has
been ravaged
by volcanoes
for thousands
of years. Can you
imagine? What
would it be like
if we had more
than one moon?
I think I like it
as it is, not too
crowded and
not too lonely
Do you remember

last week when
we saw that
skywriting and
none of us
could make out
what it said? I
saw "remember
love" but Emily
said there was
a T, and though
it didn't say
"remember to
love," I pretended
that it did. Now
it's night and I
am in bed with
a hat on. The
floor is so
cold. You are
at work, sure
to come home
smelling of
tobacco and
that spice
you put on
the fish. So
the season's
set us spinning
again, with
its new bite of

breeze. Another
year wound
round us, and
you still made
for me. Last
night I dreamt
you were that
gladiator we
joke about
in real life
gleaming in
black and gold
light, pushing
apart my
thighs. It's
electric to
think of it
now, now
that Brooklyn
has closed
down and
I'm truly
alone. I
should write
you all the
time, tell you
about this
space inside
me, like
the hollow

of a bell. But
that's not my
gift. With
you my gift
is to live, live
like this.

Anatomy

It's happened at last—
the body's become
a complete

mystery, but one
we want to get
more confused by

and will. A woman
stands on a
prairie, watching

a storm come in
her apron rippling
in the wind. Zoom in:

a skeleton floats
in busy, bloody circuitry
as an egg steps forth to say

*I'm just waiting for you
to get to know me.*
We've got to keep building

without a floorplan
Throw open the door
of the spooky shed

and cry, *Who's there!*
No matter how many
doors we open, nothing

will shake the feeling:
There's a monster in the closet!
The only answer is

it's both easy
and hard to take
care of something living—

you've got to keep
looking at it
in the light, checking

its pupils, its soil,
its coat. If it's a
human, believe

it's wistful
and wiser than
you. It's true

that hormones prod
us, but the bright
glare off

yesterday's snow
is pure
birth.

Love #1

Strange spring weather in the middle of winter.

A man opens fire
atop the Empire State;

the mail brings a skeleton of a leaf
from my lover.

The leaf is so quiet and fragile,

can't pin it to the wall with a tack;
it would tear the leaf asunder.

Julie

You were waxy
apple cheeks
with a strange film
on top, if we could
wash it off or cut
through but we
can't because
it IS you, a waxy
apple, a woman
who sits on
her smile, is
coy about
knowing. But
the knowing has
distended into
ugly words
like ORGAN
DAMAGE
I hear them on
the phone
when I call.

Army of white
pills how did
they go down
one by one or
in one fat
mouthful it's

important to
know or it's
utterly not, what
IS important is
that you trashed
it, conked out
on life. Who
are you now, I
wonder? Tucked
into white sheets
and serviced by
silver machines
that descend from
the ceiling. Your
sister is sutured
to you, she will
never leave
you, afraid she
is you, the same
blood and bone
and the same
waxy skin.

Cut flowers
are the same
as wild ones
but different
brown along
the edges and
wilting in a
plainclothes

Jersey night.
What shall
we eat, phone's
for you, I'm
going out for
a smoke, there
are still words
that make people
jump into action
like if I said
DUCK! you'd
probably do so
but what can
we say to her
no longer a
newlywed, no
longer private,
apple of ashes
in the shadow of
life. Don't die.

Aubade

Drop by drop, the sun spreads
and makes a name for itself

amidst the filth. There are cracks
in the sidewalk, lost emblems of self,

and a melancholy rebus that smells like clover.
There'll be no voyage today, no snow peas,

no chowder, just peasants in dark suits
with walking sticks, making their way

toward an empty land, completely blotto.

Love #2

There was harmony in our midst; for a moment, it was sacred.

You told me to put an orange in my cunt, then watched me do it
with a small clementine seemingly made for that purpose.

Later you danced like an imbecile on the roof, calling yourself The Puppet.

The heroin you carried was the color of crushed camel.
I flushed bags of it down the toilet.

Once when you were comatose, I crawled on top
and looked down into a valley of sinuses.

Sat in silence. Did not pummel you awake. Did not

insist   *You promised to love me through this*

Words to a Woman

This woman oh I have seen her
I worried I was her and I was her
I was her and then I was her hair
I was her mouth and her birdie nipples

Nipples coming right at you
wagons, kabobs, sugar-dips, cannons

I was worried I was her and she
was not well, she was down, or
going down, in the bar over
a tender burger, that's when
it struck me most, it was as though
she had become wallpaper, or the meat,
or the dank wood paneling

I got jealous she loved another woman
then I made another woman cry
talking about how I love men
Somewhere I must have known
how it would make her feel

How do you love men and women if you
want to love people one at a time
or one for a very long time. Where
does the other love go. Where is
love's home. Do you love
what loves you? Do you still
love me? I love you.

You are androgynous and omnipotent,
a horse. Your words blind me, I argue
for the disorient, then flail
in the ghost of the wake. You are
talking, talking, talking to me,
to my machine, at 8:03. Severely
premenstrual. I don't pick up the phone
because I am trying to talk to you
in another way. You always need
something—cigarettes, water, lemons,
booze, green things. Mostly you needed me
but I couldn't help you. You
were wallpaper. Your hands were
balled up and blue. *I don't love you*
anymore, that's what he shouted
at you. Your big blue. Numbskull.
Picking roots. Writing the deluge.
Something is always wrong with you.

Keeping the kitchen neat
that goes there and that goes there
and OK that goes there, smoking,
staring, fancying yourself a butcher
picking out the bones out the bones
picking out the bones out the bones
mama said picking out the bones mama say
find the small ones the chokers make that
slab of fish smooth and pink one long
pulsing incandescent piece of flesh
boneless loveless beautiful fish
cold fucking fish

50

We say we have a romantic friendship
but all that means is I don't understand
anything I feel, for years I thought
when we touched it would be perfect
but I had to make you stop, you were
so much rougher than I thought. Now
I want to write an epic about you and him
an epic of tennis courts and spilt blood
and big fish-eyes crying all day all night
rolling over each other one skinny one fat
in the white house like a globe of glass
in the suspended globule of bed
suspended music of blue
the door always closed, you and he
always in bed, except when
you sleepwalked into my lover's bed
and he didn't know the difference

The epic at hand seems not to know itself
Who are you, I ask of it, I am the true blue
I am the answer I am the jealous link
in the chain. You were women,
you were women.

It's not fair to make you women
not women like I like women
skinny and fat women
I wanted breasts to smother me
breasts that smelled like the inside of body
breasts that leak body, not skinny calves
or bony arms, though I love those too

You lost the weight, it dropped from you
To watch a body losing itself, to watch
it obliterate itself—it isn't you, it doesn't
even look like you. You had lovers
when you were fat I remember in
the big house you were like a queen
a boy scaled the building for you
crept over the overhangs it was gothic
it was a dream, it was all a dream:
the plastic fruit, the revolving spice rack,
the summer, the nakedness in the waterfall,
the Polaroids, the one-eyed fish.

I'm harshest on the ones I love most
just like my momma just like her momma
who picked when they wanted to teach joy
I want to give you joy
I want joy, joy, untarnished joy

You knew no boundaries
you swelled up into that house
you are the girl that can't come out
pick up your head get out of the house
nothing else can come out, the way you wear that house
you wear that house as if it were your blouse
take a step and pop goes the house

You who are so vastly desirable I could never understand
why the whole world wasn't in love with you
You bleed out onto everything, the knitting edges
knitting with other edges, the paper unfolding
an endless silver slice of origami

ink blurring the edges of letters and lips
sores running together on your breast
sores making a river

I don't love you anymore, that's what he shouted at you

Love for you, lost, love for women, lost
left to dream about the silver parts
boneless loveless beautiful fish
cold fucking fish

In the bar you cry to me, how could I have chosen
the rejection of a man over the love of a woman
Good God, I want to scream, we're speaking a script

Just push the matter through, change it
from the inside, the inside-out
Pull the man out, see the world with eyes re-shuttered

Then float me in a grove a shady grove
where no lone shoe suggests a sad story

There we'll find what's left of love
and that part of its job is to separate us

This is not your story
these are just words
words I am giving to you

I want to give you back you

tell my momma, joy, tell my momma, joy
tell my sisters and tell my momma, joy

Words to a woman, joy

Sunday

You work ten
hours in a hot
kitchen, then

sit at the bar and
have a little gin.
I know how

it is. Don't
misunderstand
me, at least not

willfully. Some nights
when the moon
is rising outside

my gated window,
I dress up
for you. If you say

you can't see
me, for a moment
I feel unspeakably

lonely. There's
a koan I know
about a rowboat—

this rowboat smashes
into your boat
along a river

of fog. You get so
angry but then as it
floats toward you

you see there's no one
driving the other
rowboat, no one

at all. I get so tired
thinking about
these things

alone. I just want
to call the same
place home.

Maine

So thick in days
the solidity of you

I cannot really see
except in dreams

where you are equally solid
but wearing a tuxedo

You wrote your own vows!
So of course I was anxious to hear

what you came up with
on your own time, when

I am not babbling
inconclusively at you as is

my habit. We are our relations,
I've learned that much—

the king gets one
bulldozer move, the bishop

is defined by its
diagonal slide, the queen

does whatever she wants
within the structure. And so we were

beings-atop-granite-rocks
for some time, we were

forms-jutting-out-into-turquoise-water,
the lobster boats waking us

at dawn. Talk to someone
long enough in one language

and you'll find all the words
you say differently:

apricot, eleven, home
Now back in the city alone

equally tempted by substantives
and substances, I finally start

to see you, your dark
star, the dance of the flashlight

against your impossible teeth.

Valentine

When kidney water came
the color of red apples

every black flash
of your eyes

said it: want; luck;
care. Grow big

and wild in my
hands, sweet

thing. I too
will be there.

Death Canoe

Surprised by blood passing
a large clot for morning
Surprised later in the day
by the ice-cold commitment
to dispersal in which I'm drowning
Eschew a gravesite once and then
there's nothing to go back to
In this sense alone I'm after something
The pitch of a nameless stream
where we dumped pitted bones
It's a part of everybody's story
and also a part of mine. I saved a handful
without knowing why. Now I'm afraid—
will they continue to decay?
Have I ill-treated them, left
them like wine in the sun?
You know I'd drink it anyway,
the curdle, the pitted bones
in freshwater. After you slice up
the greens and reds and silty mushrooms
they look fancy and it's right
that we say grace and commence
After eating we fall back on our pillows
and talk of times when the stars
were insane—children, messengers,
dalliances of light, could-be-already-dead
light, and we, the dupes. The dupes
don't mind a good night to die,

a pitch-black ride through
the Indian countryside, the driver
slapping on and off his lights
freezing women with bundles
along the road; or a descent down
a mountain in Spain, straddling sangría,
Patrícia, two wide dusty lanes. But
by morning everything's changed
It's America over and over again
I pour old wine down the drain
hoping it hasn't lodged or scarred
before I become, or we become,
or before more clots mark
the wetness of our days. On Sunday
we napped, just dropped off,
blown out by bars of sun.
You were there, I was there.
I wasn't unhappy, I wasn't scared.
I want you to know
I conducted a war for this,
a war to lose my life. I lost it,
I lost it. I reduced it to
a death canoe
and it still came out
as life.

III.

The Latest Winter

My friends play beautiful music and call it
A Cabin in the Woods. *It's so sad*
I don't even want to go there
a reviewer wrote. I live
here. Some people play the flute
The flute makes me mute, its round
holes, sound of morning that's
coming. It's dark in here tonight, just
the scalloped string of Christmas
lights and a blue slit under
the front door. Yesterday while doing
the dishes I looked closely at a fork
and saw all the crud that collects
between the tines, dried egg yolk
from days before, dark yellow and hard
What you don't know
You put it in your mouth
It's quite shocking, really, like when
I first saw that my face was made
of yellow light and dough
Big wet flakes of snow
float into the windshield
A whole host of ghosts
I have abandoned beautiful
people. To think of it is like
coming upon an air pocket—
the plane shakes and I start to panic
but then it stops and I fall asleep.

I've wasted twenty-eight years
not feeling magic, that's what
she told me, her wrists heavy
with new bracelets. It's true,
there's not much about the way
I'm living that makes me feel red
or sweaty. And if you keep watching
the flakes instead of the road
you may crash the car
but they are so very pretty!
And the snowstorm at large
can be dangerous and ugly.
Then there's the dream
in which you come back to me
bright-eyed and drug-free
but you love someone else
I wake with a jagged feeling
from my chin to my heart
which is only interrupted
by a call from my mother
who wants to talk about
my taxes. *Is life just a series*
of good dinners? she asks.
I want to ski off into the white
white moguls against the white mountain

> Take the jump can't get
> my powdersuit down
> to pee in the woods but I want
> to show him I can do it too
> Go on the gondola with Jack

he's got cognac in a flask
Can't feel my toes look for the T-bar
hold on up the steep slope
spit on the black figures below
and sing You Light Up My Life
with Emily, top of our lungs
Later at night all the adults
play Charades, I watch them
from the kids' room upstairs
My dad pretends to be Dolly Parton
by cupping his hands to his chest
They laugh in the gold light
They are all married
Outside lies the dark hill
where he dug a trail for us
to sled and the hollow moon

The candle I got for my birthday
smells like lilac and a warm baby
somewhere wants attention
What's not to like about that?
he asks. I am licking the air
open-mouthed just as you do
when you play your instrument
Yes the dissonance is truth,
whether it is killing me or not
is not relevant, as I am trying
to write without knowing
who I am. A basket of mushrooms
A quiet child drawing a tree
Drops of jade on a string

No one really knows, certainly not
the writers of the manifestos
Ask the houseplants struggling
to live through the latest winter
Or the sliver of space between
the stove and fridge
At 9am the neighborhood
gets angry, people honk
At 3pm the kids get out
of school and scream
The cops treat them
like criminals. At 11pm
I lose my mind, a room
of clacking marionettes,
a happy animal. To be frank,
my muse left town and is much happier now
She's somewhere up north
stomping snow off her boots, wiping
the glaze of a woman from her lips
and driving a rusty Volvo
I'm still here, lilac air itching
my eyes, dark pink tulips
looking up like cups. I'm still
here, sitting in my spot, the color
of claret, fingering the mold
on the folder. Maybe I should go find
the monk with copper hair, her bangs
cut high across her head
Follow her through the stone arches
made from millennia of ocean waves

Then through the garden
buzzing with yellow wheat
The TV camera films her
looking over the cliff
into the sea, she says
she doesn't have a clue, that's why
why she's qualified to be a priest
What's cruel and unusual
is so many things, the animals we eat
taste rich with their fear
So pierce through me, if you're in the mood
My braid is so thick you could paint
a picture with it, so let's do it
Just dip my head in egg and pigment
and drag it across the page
It smells good, that's the whole point
she said when she handed the candle to me

Bright open tuning

Eyes feasting on light

Who were you, emptied out   still brooding over the nest

Who was I

Before the keloid scar, the panting

A family of dream feelings is always close by me

In the pine woods a man in a burgundy parka is still
      digging a trail for saucers

He has two children he loves, his heart filling with blood

Oh my friend it's a fine and fair fiction

And my god is not holding it at all

When I was 23, I thought I'd seen some things

The inside of a truck   A madman   Afternoon
    sun on the bed

Suddenly I get it

You can suffer happiness too, for what it's worth

You can handle yourself gently

Last Day at the Office

The first thing I did was toss out
the spiced Christmas tree hanging
in the rented car, in an attempt

to restore the smell of you
to the air. The road said: Get there
any way you can. The huge new leaves

along the parkway told me:
Walk softly, as if on sawdust,
a bed of it. I'm trying to forget

the chase that's still on in the creepy streets
where we simply couldn't get enough
of the herbed gin, it was so aromatic and crisp

In a sense, I'm older now, now that
the red trident maple is jabbering unto
itself, un-snowed. Who could have known then

that the last frost of spring
was still coming, or that it would
coat everything with blue faces.

Motor Inn

No reason to be lonely, not in
this era. Creaks from the room
next door, the hollow sound
of their water. Regis Philbin
on TV, the swish of wet traffic
on the highway. Once I thought
I might be lonely, then I knew
my mind would always talk
to me. Swollen-up brain pushing
against its bone bracket.
Mysterious neighbors at
the Middletown Motor Inn.
It's 2001. No reason
to let myself in.

Walk on Campus

Why not indulge in it
A walk through the old

campus, blue humps
of snow, the street-

lamps so ice-cold
I'm on my way home

from a show I went to alone
A Korean shaman

dressed in a white napkin
got down on all fours

and slithered around the floor
invoking the goddess Yemena

It was womanly
There's the dark field where I watched

the girl I loved play rugby
There's the place on the path

where we passed awkwardly
It could be one of those nights

You're asleep and I've gone out looking for a smoke
I'm a terrible addict but I don't want you to know

But really I quit years ago. The trees creak
with the weight of yesterday's angry little snow

Sometimes the blobs fall off the white birches
and go splat and splat and splat

on the cement path. There's where
the cemetery just erupts

on top of the hill. There's the planetarium
with its roof rolled open

Such a dark square hatch, and too late to fall in

5 Huber

for Christina

Sunlight falls, finally
on the ice. On the cacti

squished in a dish, on
the rice in glass beakers.

Tree trunks slick with
water, the white dog up

on the heater. It's just like they said—
clouds give way to sun

by mid-morning, icicles make blue shadows
on the mounds. The mean steel edge of yesterday

is peeling off, the entire cul-de-sac
choppy with hunks of ice

scraped off cars. Your yellow boots
sitting quietly in the hall. Thank God

I don't have to share this morning
with anyone, not the neighbor

with his lime-green shutters, not
the mailman who left his footprints

in the snow. Is anyone
ever alone.

The Earth in April

You wanted me to be

    overwhelmed by magnolia

and so I was, fat white buds

    perched

like flocks frozen

    a moment before flight

It's spring, you whispered

    She's going to be alright

Spring in the Small Park

Taking time off to do some "dwelling"
Sky as sky as sky as sky

"Because I'm a MOMMY, that's
why," a woman tells a child

in an attempt to shut it up.
Meanwhile, beyond

the sandbox, a little girl
pokes a pigeon with a stick

but she doesn't call it cruelty
so neither will I. I know

I'm mortal. I know
how little I've built.

White flecks of dogwood float
into the pages of my book

Goodbye words

Hello milk

Goodbye at the start of summer

for J. S.

You said, I want to make it as easy as possible
for you to come back.

I appreciate that.

I walked out into a bright violet color
and it was warm, no wind coming in

off the water.

July

Hot night, my hair rich
with the smell of me
and able to grow

in the grave. It's all
I want to think about,
but everywhere I go

the music is too loud;
I guess the beautiful people
like the vague emotions

that come from big sound.
In what ways is death
like a dream? I think

I need to hear that song
again, the one you wrote
on my three remaining strings

Summer Rain

The day's sick, or I'm sick
of it—sky hard-boiled like an egg
cooked too long. I woke up
smudged onto this day, no choice:
Get up and build a biscuit.
Read Merrill, Rich, and Bishop.
Meanwhile the sky is finally
darkening to puce, the traffic
getting a swish. I wanted
more than this, and I may get it:
the pizza boys are putting
frisbees over their heads,
the men from the social club
are moving under the awning
to watch the rain try to come down
from a sky cracked with
an awful gold light, a light
like pressed smog. From upstage
right, a deep grumble: enter the sound
of water pinging on the ancient
air conditioner. All day long
I've sat at home wearing a dress
over pants, a look I kind of like
but am too embarrassed to wear out.
Now the strange white rain is souring
the flags across the way (America
on top of Puerto Rico, both tattered
and limp). It's always so hot here, here

where I live, in the attic off the baby-blue
landing, with its perpetual halo of
white neon lighting. My neighbors below
are a cute couple: the girl changed her name
from "Borsheim" to "batch" for her art; the boy Iván
smokes tons of gorgeously lush-smelling pot. Pong, pong,
the children start to scream, I like it, the angry
angry rain, gray shadows, gray gossamer.
I don't want to write like James Merrill
but I must admit I don't have his gift. Oh well,
what does one have, what can one make,
three months of no summer poems, just sitting agape.
It's not that I lack a work ethic, I work
too much—that new breed of girls
with their thin-strapped shoes
and cell phones and bad cigarette breath
are always ordering me around. Standing
apart from them one wonders
what on earth is a straight woman.
"The only love I have ever felt
was for children and other women.
Everything else was lust, pity, self-hatred,
pity, and lust." Thank you, Adrienne,
thank you very much. But there's
no refuge in any other human, or not
that I've found. "What's wrong with
self-pity, anyway," Elizabeth Bishop
writes, as the boiled sun comes
back out, the rain's over as soon as
it's begun. That's the thing about
summer rain, it always moves on

Kaspar Hauser

You thought he shot himself, but it turns out
it is his father, his torturer,
who comes back to do him in.

You remember the crispy fields
of wheat, and Kaspar working in the garden
with a priest. I remember the mean

children, and the many scenes of
language acquisition. In the end
we see handprints on the stairs

made of blood, then a shot
of the meat of his mind
getting sliced up. Afterwards

I tell you: I don't have fears
that I may cease to be; I have
a horror. Here it comes again—

the awful feeling
of being born into
a container.

After all the waiting
and non-waiting

we felt ourselves enter
with a crack, twice-

sobbed, while
everyone else knew

we had been there
all along, been

here. Here, where
we cannot & do not

see "what we are." What
do you believe in

most, I ask myself
as I fall asleep, just so

I can try to imagine
its inverse

as being true.

Report from the Field

What's new
is this white chunky coating
on my tongue

It's the taste of fear
& metal & lost people

I first saw it that day
I ran to your house
with a T-shirt wrapped
around my head

It was one of your T-shirts
so it smelled good
I held it against the sky
that was darkening

When I arrived I had to wipe
the coating off my tongue
with tissues, then with my nails
It was the souls of people
I think it was the souls of people

It happened again when I first went down
to the site, people were taking pictures
of the infernal nest, and I could taste
the metallic foam caking my tongue

Captain Joe says, there are no file cabinets,
no computers, no desks, so you can only imagine
what happened to the humans
Humans are so soft, Captain Joe says

For the first time I wondered
if this were indeed a shadow life
and the real people were living
somewhere else, where there are no words
like "dirty nuke" or "chemical soup"

But you don't refuse to breathe do you
and breathe we do, one after another
I dream that I am smoking and smoking
my lungs full of wet black leaves

I am so tired of seeing throngs of angry men in any country.
In Mohammed Atta's will: "I don't want pregnant women
or a person who is not clean to come and say goodbye to me;
I don't want women to go to my funeral or later to my grave."

I am so tired of clean and unclean
I am so tired of you hating your birth
We were all born in slither
We all came out like beautiful, glistening turds

Excuse me, I have to close the door, I say to the four guys
eating burgers at the restaurant where I work
People are complaining about the smell, I explain
They look at me strangely, as if
they still haven't heard

I don't want to meet with other poets, hear their lyrics and
        lukewarm politics
I don't want to go to academic teach-ins to discuss it
I don't want to write something pro- or anti-american
I don't want to write a eulogy

All I want to say is
I breathed you, we all breathed you
We breathed the souls of people
I think it was the souls of people

Dear Lily

11/12/01

The vines that hang out
on the cream concrete
turned scarlet today &
another black plume of smoke
reached up from our city. As if
to mitigate the perfect weather
some big silver clouds arrived, then
headache. O to loll in indifference
instead of this anxious care
What was the fall of no toilet paper
is now the fall of no survivors
No survivors   No survivors
Little shreds of my so-called
world-view begin to float off
into a deep inner space. You & I
are both filling our minds with
the same garbage, names of sauces,
lines like "one minute for your tomato"
and yes, dream is just one letter
away from dread. We dream hard,
the same hard dream, worship
& despise its power. Yet it's
hard to talk about love when I think
about all the women who live with
their cunts sutured shut, to kill
the red pulsing pleasure. Last night
my sister went to the ER because a moth

crawled in her ear—she could hear its wings
flapping deep inside her. It was sad,
she said, because she could tell
it was dying. The doctor flooded it out
with water. I wanted to tell you that, Lily,
tonight when the poets are gathering
& 265 more people are in the air,
dead. I so wish you were here, to lay
your ear against mine, hear
the hollow flapping in my head

The Future

To what do I owe
this achy wanting

life to be an envelope
of good-smelling heat, followed by

a dip in a pool of floating ice
War of icicles on red skin

After unbuttoning her
angora blend, I dream

I go through the fabric hole
into the future, which is

Hell. The buildings are black
with soot, and everything is

endlessly powered
by oil. We all have national

ID cards, but rapists are
on the loose. Far below

our high-rise, sepia vehicles
streak by. I close my eyes

but I can't find that road, the road
I've driven so many times before:

Accelerate out of the curve
Hug the red rocks on the right

O half-circle of blinding
ocean light, once I was spilled

onto that mountain. Deeper
into the dream now there is no

night, only the sick glow
of cherry lights, and the sun

when it comes
insists on melting everything.

December 23, 2001

It's amplified, this feeling,
I know. 6 Christmas trees left

at the sidewalk sale below. If
the city's our body, our feet

got blown off. At night
the wound eerily glows—

a low cloud of blue light recedes
as the cab speeds across

the bridge, taking me
home. Does sorrow have

its particular genius, or only
its sorry hole? *Only 2 more*

Borscht days 'til Christmas!
I remember when I wanted

to live alone. It's amplified,
this feeling, I know.

In a war

I'm not going to write anything out of guilt, I mean grief
I just want to know where the air becomes sky. You and I
are going to die, and I don't really care if I leave
any poems behind. There's a whiskery feeling
at the back of my throat, an evil friend. It's not
a metaphor. There's a green vein under my right eye
that will only get greener as I become more
lucid, a paper umbrella against the sun
I am not sure I know how to love
anyone. Sometimes I think there's real cruelty
in space, sometimes in my greedy little hands.
I want to think the end of everything will be
a relief, but I don't really want humans
to fail. Sometimes I care more for vegetable
than animal, or more for animal than
human being. But humans ARE animals
I eat an animal I breathe pure sky. What if
when we die we don't get it yet? I'm on the wrong track
and I know it, I bucked the lavender eye pillows
so I could keep watching the News
I can't help it, the News helps me eat, I feel
like a citizen. I "know" what's going on.
In a war you've got to make split decisions,
but even then disobedience can be genius.
Even the generals say so. I feel angers
but they are far away, embers under
a black sheet. I'm guilty, so fucking
guilty, and going out into the street

Silence

I keep seeing the moon
emerge from a pouch
of gold fog. I describe it

in my mind; sometimes
that's enough. One by one
sounds come on parade:

loud rap for the duration
of each red light, then
the soft gathering

of a motor. A skateboard
clatters by, unattached
to its owner. During the day

a man sits below my window
and sells ices. Few people
buy. He honks a black rubber horn

whenever a potential customer
walks by. Today I went down
and told him my baby upstairs

can't sleep through the noise;
it was a lie. The baby, I suppose, is
my mind. It too wants to be shameless

and hungry. After my shower
the moon had risen and was diffuse
on the window from the steam.

I would have liked to bathe in its light
but I admit I was afraid of falling. It's too late now
to tell you about my flight over the Atlantic,

over Godthab—the words are gone. Though
I can still see my mother sleeping next to me
like a child, her lipstick bleeding out along

her beautiful new wrinkles. She admits
she was never very maternal: "Some mornings
I lay in bed thinking, If I have to spend another day

playing with Barbies, I'll die." I came home that night
and took everything off my walls, laid my sea rocks
in a spiral. It's time to know something

about the art of living. The sound of traffic
inexplicable as the taste of milk, it just IS
and haunts me. I already got a glimpse

of tomorrow's paper:
How Scared Should We Be?
Skullcap is a bitter brew but

I drink it to sleep in one
chunk. I always brew it too long, then
take the tea bag out with a pair

of kitchen tongs, the kind
you told me to buy. You said
I'd never be sorry. You were right.

Dailies

Little sneaky fires
in my fingers. In my
wrinkle, the privileged one.

Groups of people
coagulate, make sounds.
They don't want

to be called
evil. Who does.
The western window

makes quite a show
of it, a blanket of
magnificent yellows

demands everything
of me. No book for a human
to tell it how to be.

She says she despises
the daily, how can it be?
Little fire fingers can't tell

a fever, they cry wolf
like today's terrorist alert.
Front page of the paper,

more brown faces.
Fussy chemicals come in
with the dusk. In another time

this would have been
inspiration. A quiet morning
feels dangerous, but so does

a loud one. A child straps on
her backpack, gets ready
to know. If I say: *It is despair, precisely*

well that just makes it precise.
I want to feel like I had a hand
in it, making the world.

ZED

Zed is a platform for marginalised voices across the globe.

It is the world's largest publishing collective and a world leading example of alternative, non-hierarchical business practice.

It has no CEO, no MD and no bosses and is owned and managed by its workers who are all on equal pay.

It makes its content available in as many languages as possible.

It publishes content critical of oppressive power structures and regimes.

It publishes content that changes its readers' thinking.

It publishes content that other publishers won't and that the establishment finds threatening.

It has been subject to repeated acts of censorship by states and corporations.

It fights all forms of censorship.

It is financially and ideologically independent of any party, corporation, state or individual.

Its books are shared all over the world.

www.zedbooks.net
@ZedBooks